The Poetry of Social Work

The Poetry of Social Work

Shelley A.Wyckoff

authorHOUSE®

AuthorHouse™
1663 Liberty Drive
Bloomington, IN 47403
www.authorhouse.com
Phone: 1-800-839-8640

Published by AuthorHouse   06/04/2012

ISBN: 978-1-4678-5630-0 (sc)
ISBN: 978-1-4678-5629-4 (e)

Library of Congress Control Number: 2011960084

CONTENTS

Afternoon Idleness

The music is so soothing to my ears.

Every bone in my body moves just right to each beat
of the drum and whine of the saxophone.

Every sound is in my head as I let my body have its
way . . .

Moving up and down and all around

Sweet smells of cinnamon tease my nose as I spot
the cinnamon candle still burning on the coffee table.

Soft leather sofas with velvet pillows catch my eye as
I fall into their softness.

AIDS Where Did You Come From?

John was blond, blue-eyed, tall, kind and gentle . . .
Set my soul on fire and . . . Made my body explode like rockets.
A dynamic lover . . . A dynamic lover he was.

Dan looked like my favorite actor. Smelled of Cool Water and
sometimes Drakkar Noir.
Finger nails clean and shaped to perfection.
A wonderful lover . . . A wonderful lover he was.

And then Bob with deep penetrating eyes.
Shirts starched and ironed to perfection.
Valuable gifts he gave me.
An excellent lover . . . An excellent lover he was.

And Sam, who was black as midnight,
Voice as smooth as silk
Declared his love for me and no other.
Constant undivided attention, he gave me.
A superior lover . . . A superior lover he was.

And many, many others like them . . . with similar profiles filled my
days and nights with mystical sexual bliss.

Now . . .
My skin sags and my hair is thin.
Few pounds have I.
Sores I can't hide and
endless pain to endure . . . .
AIDS . . . .
Where did you come from?

Alcohol Amateur

It's been a long week
Ready and anticipating my 2-day release
Trying desperately to get twisted so
I can finally be in peace
'Til today, I spent most of my days sober
Thinking this as I'm riding in my girl's Nova
Realizing we had to hurry cause
Liquor store hours were almost over

I see a hobo eyeing me kinda strange
But still he got his hand out looking for some change
Stale cigarettes, urine, alcohol, and vomit
All rushed my nostrils like a raging comet

But as I stepped through the door,
I suddenly felt like a kid in a candy store
So many proofs, so many flavors,
With white and brown concoctions that change your
behavior
I'm not a pro at this so what should I select?
Alize, E&J, or a bottle of Moet?
I guess I'll go ahead and holla at my girl Brandy
But damn, that 20 I left at home sure would've come in handy

Distracted by folks talking about blazing
While trying to explain my order to the Asian I
had decided on purchasing a bottle of Henn
Not even listening to the man behind the counter
Saying for me to come again
Pausing, it made me think as I looked
Down at the bottle in my hand
Was it his master plan to first addict
And ultimately ruin the black man?

All In A Day

The white coats are like family to me
White coats here . . . White coats there . . .
Drawing the red stuff from the Tired . . .
Tired trenches
Missing one trench and trying another
Invasive procedures . . . Invasive Procedures
All in a day . . . All in a day . . .

Privacy . . . Privacy . . . long gone
Broken down submission to the protocol
Dependent on others . . . dependent on others . . . Try
this . . . try that . . . try it all . . .
All in a day . . . All in a day . . .

Body image . . . Nowhere to be found—From lean
to bones
Autonomy . . . Long gone . . . as the pills do their thing
Powerlessness . . . Helplessness . . . Loss of control . . .
Shoulders bound down like heavy shackles from stressors . . .
Dark shadows over take any faint light
All in a day . . . All in a day . . .

Night turns to day and day turns to night . . .
Light from darkness seem no where in sight . . .
Mumbling . . . mumbling . . . mumbling . . .
Whispers . . . whispers . . . whispers . . .
All about me . . . All about time . . . All about me . . .
Self-esteem down and almost gone . . .

Hold those tears . . . hold those tears . . .
Loneliness . . . anger . . . self pity . . .
Not permitted . . . Not recognized . . . useless . . .
Feelings locked away like a sealed bottle . . .
All in a day . . . All in a day

America's Changing Colors

No feelings
No understanding
No love . . .no equality . . . no fairness
Color me American
Color me American
No vision
No hearing
No listening
No giving
Color me American
Color me American
No sharing
No peace
Color me American
Color me American

Another Mother

Mother, madame, ma-ma, mu-dear.
My solid rock . . . My protector . . . My Madonna . . . My
apple pie ala mode . . . My fairy in a fairy tale . . . My
caviar and aged Chablis.
Mother, madame, ma-ma, mu-dear.
A princess in disguise. A wolf in sheep's clothing
waiting to take my very soul. . Leaving my mind like a
puzzle with a thousand pieces . . . Powerless against
you and your spell
Mother, madame, ma-ma, mu-dear.
Our secret weighs me down like tons of metal. Your
touch once warm-now makes me cringe. Eyes that
once said love, now say lust . . . Ears that once listened
are now deaf to my cries as I loudly scream for
another mother . . . I want another mother . . . I need
another mother.

As the World Turns

As the world turns, we find the same . . .AIDS,
substance abuse, sexually abused children,
neglected children, violence against men,
violence against women, gay bashing
homophobia, parent/child conflict, health
problems, homelessness, troubled youth,
pregnant children, death and dying, social
injustice, economic injustice, inequality, and
disharmony

Everywhere . . . . They are
everywhere
As the World Turns

Ask Me

I know the numbers to the state employment
office, welfare services, food stamps office,
church food pantries and community emergency
relief programs.
Ask me . . . 'cause I know
I washed dishes for two days, cleaned houses
for three, washed windows and cut yards.
Ask me . . . 'cause I know
Eviction notices are sent by landlords.
Water, lights and gas are long gone.
Ask me . . . 'cause I know
I feel like a failure 'cause I can't make ends
meet.
I can't sleep and my headaches are stinging.
My stomach ache like a dagger has been
plunged.
Ask me . . . 'cause I know
I've seen the smile-less faces, and heard the
chilly voices
Ask me . . . 'cause I know

At the Social Work Conference

All shades of colors, sizes and shapes. Different
agendas and different issues.. the healthy and the
unhealthy, gathering at the social work conference.
Lots of money—little money—no money . . .
New clothes—old clothes—no clothes
Hair up—hair down—hair twists
Nappy hair, straight hair, no hair.
gathering at the social work conference.
All sleeping, some sleeping, half sleeping
Coffee drinkers, water drinkers, liquor drinkers. Buffet
eaters—trying to eat their money's worth. Others
sharing secrets about their programs and about
faculty they wish they didn't have . . gathering at the
social work conference.
Some focus on rest and relaxation, others shop 'til
they drop and see the sights. Still others shop, give
gossip and receive gossip. Networking and job
seeking—a priority,
gathering at the social work conference.
Sessions, sessions and more sessions
Sessions about curriculum and standards
Sessions about poor folks, gay folks, dying folks and folks in
general . . . Sessions about gatekeeping,
oppression and empowerment. Some boring and
others dynamic—All at the social work conference.

Bad News

The Sound of Laughter—Oh No!
Fireworks—Oh No! Tears of Joy—Oh No!
Cause . . . I was bad news.

Collecting all the blues and pinks—Oh No!
Shopping for necessities—Oh No!
Choosing a name to fit me—Oh No!
Cause . . . I was bad news.

Checking each hour for the sign of life—Oh No!
Jumping for glee at the slightest move—Oh No!
Regular exams by the white coats—Oh No!
Cause . . . I was bad news.

Starving and more starving—Oh Yes!
Drugs you took that you shouldn't have—Oh Yes.
Hard falls on the floor . . . you welcomed—Oh Yes!
Punching your stomach until it was black & blue—
Oh yes!

Cause . . . I was bad news, I was bad news

Beautiful

I opened my eyes this beautiful morning
and thanked God for the beautiful sun
as I crawled out of my beautiful bed
and looked at the beautiful trees
and heard the beautiful birds singing.
I went to my beautiful bathroom
to take a beautiful bath
and to brush my beautiful teeth
and put on my beautiful clothes.
Then I greeted my beautiful husband
with a beautiful smile,
and gave him a beautiful kiss,
and made us a beautiful breakfast.
I went outside to my beautiful yard
and got in my beautiful car
and drove down my beautiful street
and passed by some beautiful cars.
I had beautiful thoughts as
I went to my beautiful job
and parked in front of my beautiful building and went into my
beautiful office
and saw my beautiful clients waiting to be helped.

Because It Was Profitable

Many houses went . . . the subsidized and unsubsidized
Those with windows and without windows.
Roofs and porches with holes.
The small, the large, the painted and unpainted downed by
big machines that whined from sunrise to sunset
because . . . it was profitable.

The little dance hall where we danced with joy.
The café where everybody knew everybody.
The neighborhood store where credit wasn't an issue.
The poolroom where problems were solved, they all went . . .
because . . . it was profitable.

The chicken coop that sold the spicy chicken, barbecue that
fell off the bones, pickled pig feet and dill pickles . . . . they all
went . . .
because . . . it was profitable. because . . . it was profitable.

Because

Because
I don't need much sleep
I don't need much money
I like bureaucratic agencies
I like meeting people
I like interviewing people

Because
I like carrying a beeper
I like transporting children
I like testifying in court
I like helping child abusers
I like getting out of my bed at 2 a.m. to pick up abandoned
children
I like helping batterers
I like being hit and cursed

Because
I like helping depressed people
I like fighting racist people
I like problems and more problems
I like being overworked
I like to talk
I like to write
I do it all . . . Because . . . I like being a social worker.

Black Girl and Self-esteem

Black Girl . . . Black Girl . . . Black Girl
Oh . . . Beautiful Black Girl!
Justify nothing for there's nothing to justify
Apologize not for your ebony hue and thick hair.
Apologize not for your full lips and shapely hips.
Hold your head up towards the sky.
Square your shoulders.
Let not foulness flow from those beautiful lips.
Let not men of statue and non-statue dominate you.
Let not creatures of the street define your direction.
Affirm, Affirm, Affirm your goodness and royal linage.
Demand, insist, scream loudly that you are a Black Girl,
Black Girl, Black Girl . . . deserving of nothing but the best.

I Fall Real Short As A Father

I did not . . .
mold the moral character and values of my child
provide adequate food, clothing and shelter for my child
show love to my child
protect my child
bond emotionally with my child
connect with my child and
make a safe place for my child
I Fall Short . . . Real Short.

I did not . . .
develop the spiritual intelligence of my child
teach my child to pray
teach my child the skills of making a living
model integrity and ethical behavior
support my child during disappointments and hard times
develop my child's problem-solving ability
I Fall Short . . .Real Short.

I did not . . .
teach my child to be kind
teach my child to be respectful
teach my child to be generous
teach my child to accept differences
I Fall Short . . . Real Short . . . As A Father

Black Women

They care for the young, the old, the sick, the healthy, the needy.
Some are cooks, teachers, farmers and factory workers.
Others are shopkeepers, maids, faith healers and seamstresses.
Some are sisters, daughters, aunts, cousins, wives and live-ins.
Some are social workers, psychologists and listeners.
Some are old-fashioned, pitiful and firm. They are gentle, hard, humble and caring. They are brave, conscientious and resilient.
They are black women . . .

Bondage

Herded in like cattle
Intertwined and chained like a chain-link fence
Stripped of outer and inner layers
Zero privacy
Numbers instead of names
Consumed by self-blame and self-pity
Anger overtakes the soul

Adults return to child-like stage
No more self-determination and thinking for self
Humiliation and emptiness
Powerlessness, oppression and frustration

Submissive and rebellion
Needs ignored
It's all about bondage

Botanical Garden of Diversity

We are the millions of flowers of colors abounding,
blooming and growing
Lots of loving—little loving—no loving
Lots of gain—some gain—no gain
Superiority at will . . . Energy and creativeness
Lack of interaction and frivolous play
Exploitation, discrimination, victimization, oppression
Hatred passed down from generations . . . . fighting for
resources
Abuse abounding, Living in harmony—an unreachable goal
Depriving each other of sun and rain
Problems in relationships
Problems in communication
Problems in environment
Overwhelming hate crimes
Epidemic of stigma and stereotypes
The welcome wagon—we never saw
Universal human needs unrecognized In this gigantic
Botanical Garden of Diversity

Changes

Life's changes are like . . . sailing through blue, calm
waters with a peacefulness unmatched.
Beauty and serenity surround me.
My mind mellows with distractions,
then . . . peacefulness disturbed by powerful unruly
waves, tossing the boat in all directions lasting what
seems like an eternity . . . Then greatness and
thankfulness.
Then another jolt that seems endless . . .
seconds, days, weeks, months, years
Calm, then volatile, calm again, then volatile.. Ups
and downs . . . harmony . . . ups and downs . . .
harmony . . . ups and downs . . . then harmony again
Changes . . . Changes . . . Changes

Color Me

No feelings
No understanding
No love
No equality
No fairness
No vision
Color me . . . American
No hearing
No listening
No giving
No sharing
No peace
Color me American . . . Color me . . . A-mer-i can . . .
Color me . . . Non-American

Distressed . . .

Wordlessly I stare around me . . . I crumble like a
puzzle dropped . . . My face shows the bite of winter's
teeth and the sting of summer's heat . . . No peace nor
contentment have I known.
Hunger is like a mother to me—clinging, clinging.
Rockets shoot throughout my body . . . Emptiness and
pain controls my mind . . . as my thoughts are forced
to stand still.
As this pain pierces me time and time again . . .
dreariness is all I know and feel. The sun is shining,
but I'm cold. My heart is like lead, my soul troubled.
Sadness, is my clone. A smile is like a stranger to me
Finally, the words come . . . Why me? Why me? Why
me?

Face of Steel

You don't know that . . .
I have just been fired from my job, the rent is due,
utilities are off, and the fridge is empty because I wear
the face of steel . . . .
You don't know that . . .
my drug test was positive and I was sentenced for
three years for violating drug court because I wear the
face of steel . . .
You don't know that . . .
My husband of fifty years says he loves my best
friend today, yesterday, and always and that I can
take it or leave it. You can't tell I'm feeling it because I
wear the face of steel.

Fall Down

Fall down . . . but get up
when you can't pay the bills.
when death knocks at your door.
Fall down . . .but please get up

Fall down . . ..but get up
when there are endless fights between you and an
unfaithful partner..
when the car won't crank.
Fall down . . . but please get up

Fall down . . . . but get up
When there's no food in the house . . .
Mama's lost her mind . . .
Children on drugs . . .
Fall down . . . but please get up
Fall down . . . but please get up!
P . . . l . . . e . . . a . . . s . . . e Get . . . Up

Fear

I can't hug you the way I want to hug you . . . for fear of
being seen.
I can't take you where I want to take you . . . for fear of
being seen.
I can't gaze into your eyes lovingly and longingly For
fear of being seen.
I can't run my fingers through your hair, down your
face, down your back . . . for fear of being seen.
I can't whisper my love in your ears . . . for fear of being
seen . . .
I can't move my body close to yours in rhythm . . . for
fear of being seen.
I can't take you home to meet my folks . . . for fear of being
seen.
I can't take you to my office party . . . for fear of being
seen.
I can't . . . I can't . . . I just can't . . . for fear of being
seen.

Fix My Kid

Eyes that say kill . . . Ears that refuse to hear . . . Tongue
that has a hundred ways to lash out . . . Tears that
won't form.
Fix my kid.

Arms that refuse to reach out . . . Legs that refuse to go
to school . . . Fists that hit other kids . . . Lips that curse
the teachers . . . Hands that destroy property.
Fix my kid.

Actions that disrupt the class . . . Mouth that get drunk
and swallow drugs . . . Nose that sniff glue . . . Hands
that steal . . . Heart that's cold as ice .
Fix my kid.

Declares the gang as family . . . Threatens to commit
suicide . . . Tries to burn down the house . . . Sexually
abuses other children . . . Threatens to kill mom, dad,
sister and brother.
Fix my kid . . . Fix, Fix, Fix . . . Fix my kid.
I need you to . . . Fix my kid.

For You . . . My Friend

I wish for you lots of love in your life, wisdom to make decisions, blessings, gratitude for things, smiles for others.
I wish for you joy to lift the spirit of others.
I wish for you moments of excitement to make your heart tingle.
I wish for you new adventures that bring brightness in your eyes.
I wish for you tenderness toward the oppressed and depressed.
I wish for you strength when you are tired.
I wish for you patience with the slow.
I wish for you health each day of your life.
I wish for you happiness today and tomorrow and always.
I wish for you many memories too special to forget.
I wish for you hugs whenever you need them.
I wish for you valleys and peaks so that you will see the glory of God, his love and his mercy.

Hate / Love

Oh-o-o-o-o . . . I hate you, hate you, hate you for the
pain . . . the pain . . . the pain.
I love you, love you, love you for the pleasure . . . the
pleasure . . . the pleasure.
Because of you, when I look into the mirror, I see me . . .
Cold as ice, pain before pleasure,
hatred, and violence, carelessness and
vindictiveness, bitterness, anxiety, uncertainty,
a stifled creative mind, a voice of hatred, a thirst for
revenge, a desire to maximize human suffering, and
hostility without provocation.
I see me . . . I see me . . . In the mirror. What I am . . .
I owe to you.

Hello World

I'm ready . . .
I'm ready for kisses and hugs, love, respect, and
honesty . . .for rest and sharing.
I'm ready . . .
I'm ready for basketball, volleyball and dance,
homecoming and graduation, queen and kingship,
homework and movies, Tuskegee, Yale or Spelman.
I'm ready . . .
I'm ready for sunshine and rain . . . valleys and hills . . .
sad and happy memories.
I'm here . . .
I'm here . . . I'm coming out to this big, big world . . . I'm
born!
Hello world . . .Hello world

He's Not Gone

He's not gone—he's not gone
He can't be gone
Just out for a while
Just out with a friend . . .
Cause he's got
tears to wipe,
repairs to make,
bills to pay, and
love to give.
He'll come back—I know he will
Not sure when—not sure when
But he's not gone.

Hopeful Anticipation

In my mother's womb, I feel safe, warm, loved,
beautiful, hopeful, proud, and happy
Now . . .
I dream of leaving my mother's womb to enter the
world and find beauty, warmth, pride, commitment,
love, fairness, hope, faith, and happiness.

How Many times?

How many times have I felt the whip? Because I
opened my mouth to speak, I spoke too much or too
little, I spoke too quickly or not quick enough.
How many times have I felt the whip? Because food
was not cooked, clothes were not pressed to
perfection, children not tucked in their beds, hubby
wanted an excuse to go out or if I looked at him in
bewilderment.

How many times have I felt the whip? Because he
had a hard day on the job, didn't have enough money,
couldn't pay the bills or
didn't want to pay the bills.

How many times have I felt the whip? When he turned
to the bottle, turned to drugs, turned to other women.

How many times have I felt the whip? Because a
beating is a private matter, because he was raised in
a hostile environment, because his daddy did it and
his granddaddy did it. Because it meant power, he
had to have control of his house, I was his property,
and my mama said "stay".
How many times have I felt the whip? How many
times have I felt the whip? Too many times . . . Too
many times . . . .

I Am

I am everyone and everyone is me . . .
The rainbow of races, the loved and the unloved, the boss
and the peon.
The free and the chained, the wife, the husband and the
lover, the rose, carnation and lily. The red, black, white and
yellow. The blue-collared, white-collared, no- collared. The
gay, the lesbian, the transgendered. The sister, brother,
mother, father. The son, the daughter, the cousin, aunt,
uncle. The friend, the enemy, the sexually and racially
oppressed. The strong, fragile, and disabled. The old and
the young. The depressed and the happy. The beautiful, the
ugly, and the in-between. The bold and the timid. The rural
and the urban. The doctor, the patient, the social worker,
and the client. I am, I am, I am . . .
I am everyone and everyone is me.

I Can't Compete

He consoles her when she's lonely
Sharing her inner most thoughts with him
Makes her feel like Princess Diana
Makes her feel loved like no other
And makes her neglect all others
Including the little ones. I can't compete . . .
I can't compete . . .

She sleeps with him all wrapped up
Day and night—she hangs with him
Gives him her all and more
Dependent on him for her very life
Cheat, lie, and steal to be with him. I can't compete . . .
I can't compete . . .
Because of him, her lips are wet and eyes glossy
Her eyes say that she is on a different planet
Her body sways and sways
Her temper flares when she
can't be with him
I can't compete . . .
I can't compete . . . with drugs

I Choose

I choose . . .
to be sad, to conceal my soul's true gaze, to have doubts
and fears, to stand on the shores of unhappiness, to wear
the face of anger and resentment, to be lonely and loveless,
to be abused and used, to roam with the wild and ruthless, to
lie and steal, to hide my feelings, to be selfish and
ungrateful, to be deceitful, pretentious, and treacherous.
I choose . . . I choose . . . to be miserable.

I Don't Care

I don't care if you are red,
white, brown or yellow,
skin bumpy or smooth as silk,
wear a dingy shirt and high water pants or . . .
a skirt that looks like it belongs to your daughter.

I don't care if you curse like a sailor ,
spit snuff in all directions, belch galore or
use and sell drugs.

I don't care if you dodge the landlord,
cause you can't pay the rent,
don't know your baby's daddy
and don't know your own daddy
I don't care . . . I don't care
'cause you are a human being.

I Gotta Go

Hitting me . . .
Kicking me . . .
Knocking me . . .
Raping me . . .
Sorry, but I gotta go
Sorry, but I gotta go
Cursing me . . .
Yelling at me . . .
Degrading me . . .
Hatred stares . . .
Sorry, but I gotta go
Sorry, but I gotta go
Self-esteem all gone
Food . ..I have none.
Clothes . . .tattered and torn
Job and money . . ..none
Sorry, but I gotta go
Sorry, but I gotta go . . .
I gotta go. Right now

I Like Me

I own my strengths,
my limitations, my valleys, my joys, my deficiencies, my
hate, my greed, my jealousy, my failures, my confidence,
my mountains, my pains, my gifts, my love, my generosity,
my admiration, my successes, my doubts .
I like me . . . yes, I like me.
I Like me . . .. like me . . .. like me.

I Need Help . . .I'm The Helper

My rent is due and I can't pay. The ice box is empty and my children are hungry. My mate is looking at another. My children are wayward and labeled with conduct disorders. Two DUIs are a blemish on my record. The voices are louder in my head. I hate my clients and they hate me. I don't want to learn and I don't want to do. I regret seeing the light of a brand new day. I'm the helper . . . but I need help.

I Promise

I promise . . . I promise as a social worker to help red, white, yellow, black and ebony people in need. To challenge the mighty social injustice . . . To not look the other way when oppression and discrimination prevails . . . To respect your right of privacy . . . To respect each and every person . . . To respect differences that exist in all cultures . . . To not interfere with decisions you make . . . To be your partner in the helping process . . . To point out your strengths and not just your faults . . . To not take advantage of our professional relationship . . . To be trustworthy . . . To continue to learn and grow . . .
I promise . . . I solemnly promise.

I Wanna Work

Lazy, Lazy, Lazy, Lazy
Sitting home all day and night I try to figure out the Young
and the Restless
I wanna work . . . I wanna work
My world falls apart day by day as I hear of talk of Welfare to
Work
No more sitting, and sitting, and sitting.
No more waiting for the mail man
I wanna work . . . I wanna work
Lots of things to think about
Need new clothes and shoes
Need a babysitter for my precious ones
Need a car to meet this order
I wanna work . . . I wanna work

I Wear the Scars

Conflicting images of me and myself
Feelings of inadequacy dancing in my head
Loss of self in a darkened forest . . . Living each day as a
peon
Feeling unworthy and unjustified
Needs are not legitimate
When you see me . . . You see visible and invisible scars
Scars of love gone bad and years of beatings
Scars of unfaithfulness and terror
Scars that will never go away
I wear the scars . . . I wear them well.

I Will Not Be Silent

My social work colleagues . . .
When you discriminate against people and things . . .
Disrespect ethnicity, disregard humanity,
mimic sex, joke about sexual orientation, joke about religion,
joke about mental disability, belittle physical disability, belittle
political beliefs, participate in dishonest deeds, fraud or
deception, I will not be silent . . .
I Will Not Be Silent

I Wish I Could Sit

My legs are tired—My arms heavy
Carrying heavy bags and pocketbook
   I wish I could sit

Standing in the aisle . . . I must.
Crowded together and sweating together
All of the seats in the back are taken.
   I wish I could sit

All tired eyes look toward empty seats.
Afraid to even want those seats
Waiting on each other to make a move
Crowded together and sweating together
   I wish I could sit

Strong voices from within
Affirmed and confirmed my importance
That I'm loved & loved & loved some more
By the mighty man above
A member of the human race
Living-in the home of the brave
and the land of the free
With this in mind, I took a seat.
Yes I took a seat in the front of the bus . . .
I took a seat in the front of the bus . . . .

I'm A Stutterer

They laugh at me
They mimic me
They lose patience with me as I try to express myself
My thoughts are solid . . . My words formed . . . but the words
won't come. Cause . . . Cause . . . I'm a stutterer

I'm Aching

I'm aching "for two arms, two legs "for ten fingers, ten toes
"two eyes, two ears "a brain, fortitude, wisdom, and skill.
I'm aching "to feel the wind on my cheeks "to taste the depth
of delightful dishes . . . to feel the warmth of a human touch . . . .
to accept the love that may be offered.
I'm aching . . .I'M ACHING FOR THESE THINGS AND MORE

Incarcerated Woman

I am . . .
Isolated from family and friends
Indecisive because of decisions made for me
Stigmatized by society
Lonely because I'm wrapped in darkness
Loveless because of broken promises
Joyless because of my hopeless situation
Criticized because of my immoral behavior
Abandoned by my previous relationships
Dishonest because I have learned to cheat
Deceitful because I have learned to lie
I am . . .
I am an incarcerated woman.

Invisible Shackles

Fear
Love
Insecurity
Low self-esteem
Domination
Beauty
Low paying jobs
Lack of education
Internal struggles
Secrets and
Hate
Invisible shackles are holding me down

Life

Headlights beaming in streams
Like flatliners of a deathbed
Each face wears the trials of time
Going here, there and nowhere
Faces like a maze
All moving to a different beat
All searching and looking
Racing as if in competition
Caught up in the web of life
With baggage of all dimensions.

Light My Fire

Expand my mind to the breadth and depth
of the tallest tree and widest river
with things and things and more things
with people and people and more people
with places and more places
Light my fire

Let my imagination run wild like
the colors of a kaleidoscope
the crossings of a matrix
and the falling of a thousand piece jigsaw
puzzle
Light my fire, Light my fire
So . . . that I may continue to search,
Learn and grow
Light my fire

Longing for You

I long for your hands to press my breasts
Like a pot of gold and to kiss my
Lips like a fresh sweet plum . . . ripe from the vine
I long for your eyes . . .
that are stuck on me with a big "A"
for admiration
I long for the feel of lean hard arms
that encircle and protect me . . . .
The press of your body that says get ready
your legs as they glide along mine in
preparation for an intertwine
I long for you and me and me and you
And
Us and Us

Lost Love

We wake each day . . .
silence all around us
as we walk on eggshells
and act like strangers.
We close the bathroom door
as we bathed our bodies and act like our
eyes have never viewed each others
nakedness

There is much small talk
about the children and
what they are doing, what
they need, and what they have
become.

Then more talk about the
neighbors and the relatives . . .
about news in the community, in the state and in the nation . . .
No talk of inner desires and secrets of the heart . . .
No talk of love and longing for passionate love.

Our eyes dodge each other and are
peeled to the floor.
Self-confidence diminished and
Self-esteem a thing of the past.

As the day ends, a new day begins
There is more of the same.
The wall grows higher and wider
Resentment, anger and sadness deepens
as we find a corner in one room or
another or sit in the same room
but obviously our thoughts are miles apart as we reminisce about our
lost love.

Love . . . The Best Love

I love you because . . .
You are easy as Sunday morning
You are as soothing as chicken noodle soup
You are as toasty as an electric blanket on a cold
winter's night
As mellow as cold ice cream sliding down my throat on a
hot summer day
As soft as cotton puffs and as gentle as a fall breeze
I love you . . . and you . . . and you Because you are
easy as Sunday morning

Low Down . . . Deep Down

My mind is like a cave without light
I try to get up but fall right back down
as I stumble from left to right . . . . in total darkness.
Life seems so cruel as my mind plays movies of yesterday
Yesterday's deep scars and wounds etched in my mind . . .
torturing my soul. My mind is like a twisted rope that has no
loose spots. Will this darkness end so that I can live?
I am low down . . . . . . .deep down

Missing

We have a big white house with sofas fit for a king.
Lamps that sparkle for a queen.
Beds that beg for occupants.
Bathrooms that look like lavish powder rooms.
Tables and chairs lavishly decorated.
A kitchen with the finest cutlery and cookware.
Porches that put one to sleep.
We have so much . . . so much, but yet so little.
Love is missing

Multiple Wounds

I smile from ear to ear.
I laugh so loudly its soup for the soul.
I have a hug for every person I meet.
I show excitement about each new day.
I walk with renewed energy.
I'm involved in many activities.
I dress like a fashion model.
Yes, I'm pleasing to the eye and look and act Like I'm on top
of the world . . . on the outside . . . . on the outside
                    But on the inside . . .
I have a broken spirit and I can't think straight.
My thoughts are of tragedies, disappointments, trials and
tribulations in my life.
I'm angry and fighting enemies everyday, trying to avoid
traps intentionally set for me.
Each day I'm waiting to be delivered from my multiple
wounds.
        I'm waiting for the inside to match the outside.

Never to Return

Flatliners are vivid in my mind. Family, friends, and lovers'
hearts are in tune . . . Tears fall freely like a fountain . . .
Never to return
My John Henry requested over and over "Shop for the very
best" . . . Need a box for his protection . . . Can't let that cold dirt
touch him
Never to return
Sleepless nights and food galore . . . Shadows come and go
Memories shared and shared again . . . Lots of wailing and
snotty noses
Never to return
The preacher man said many words . . . Songs and songs
galore . . . Tears drop by the buckets . . . All for my love . . .All
for you who's never to return

No Miracle

The plan sounds so beautiful . . .
More money, more food, more clothes, more self-respect,
more pride
Welfare to Work—A Miracle
Little money, little food, little clothes,
Work long hours—but little return
Still struggling—Still struggling
Welfare to Work—No Miracle

One Eye Open

I keep one eye open
for you and you and you
who talk and talk and talk
like you have jitters of the mouth
endless lies in great proportion

I keep one eye open
for you and you and you
who wear the britches so tight
and creases don't show
that even worms can't breathe

I keep one eye open
for you and you and you
who say you love me but
your penis stays soft as butter
and your eyes as distant as the North Pole

I keep one eye open for you and you and you with
smiling faces and hugs galore . . . .but eyes that say hate,
hate, hate and hands that feel like ice

Prison Without Walls

I jumped with joy as the shackles fell to the ground. No more
uniforms . . . but freedom to wear whatever I desire.
A smorgasbord of food to choose from.
Now solo showers and lingering baths.
But . . . days flow into nights . . . nights into days . . . Holes in
my shoes . . . air in my stomach . . . pain in my head.
My steady stride now a creep. Hope diminished. Sorry . . .
no jobs here . . . Where did you work for the past 5 years?
Throat dry, lips parched. Willpower—a thing of the past.
I see the reflection of a man—my reflection, who remains in
prison, But, one without walls.

Professional Credibility

Once upon a time, there was a social worker. Once upon a time, there was a social worker who believed in . . .
Diversity
Leadership
Community service
Rehabilitation
Ethical practice
Research and Competence
Once upon a time there was a social worker who believed . . .
that people could change, that love is synonymous to life, that training is important, that different strategies should be explored and that innovative interventions should be tested.
Once upon a time, there was you and me

Prom Night

When she left . . . .Her eyes radiated like bright stars full of innocence and hopeful glee . . . .A childlike smile from ear to ear . . . Hair piled high upon her head . . . each strand slicked down with royal crown . . . Elegant earbobs dangled from side to side

Long, shiny gown made just for her . . . Perfect fit that hugged her curves, leaving room for no wrinkles . . . Bow tied neatly behind her back

When she returned . . . innocent smile was no more Gown's shine had lost its bling . . . Wrinkles on the garment was like an aged face . . . The bow in the back was now upside down . . . A missing earbob never to be found . . .

Hair limp and dangling . . .

Girl to woman

on

Prom Night

Real Expectations of Social Work

Social work is about • Serving others
• Advocating for silent voices • Challenging social Injustice for vulnerable and
oppressed populations • Helping people to help themselves • Empowering the disempowered • Valuing individual differences • Recognizing strengths • Respecting cultural and ethnic diversity • Respecting clients' rights to make decisions • Promoting the well-being of clients • Engaging in continuous training for competence • Respecting clients rights to privacy • Making appropriate referrals • Participating in policy development • Seeking to ensure that all people have equal
access to resources, services and opportunities.
SOCIAL WORK is about ALL of THESE and MORE . . .

Scars

I've got scars in my mind, in my soul and on my body.
Scars in my mind from injustices
hypocrisy . . . lying . . . stealing . . . distrust . . .
Scars in my soul from backbiting . . .
insincerity . . . anger . . . love . . . betrayal . . . death.
Scars on my body from illnesses . . .
poverty . . . diseases . . . beatings . . . drugs.
I've got scars in my mind, my soul and body . . . Scars that
just won't go away . . . Scars that just won't heal . . .
When you meet me . . . You SEE and HEAR
the scars.

Secret Lover

My Secret Lover
Is a tall and handsome man,
wears Tommy Hilfiger
and smells of Drakkar Noir.
My Secret Lover
Is a devoted father, son, brother, uncle,
is peaceful and kind,
tells me that he loves me like no other.
My Secret Lover
reads the Bible and goes to church,
has a good job and
volunteers in the community.
My Secret Lover
soothes me when I'm sick,
makes me feel safe and
gives me his last dime.
My Secret Lover
slips quietly into my room,
wipes away my flowing tears
as he rips my hole apart,
taking my childhood away.

See Saw

Birds singing and talking . . . Lightheartedness all around
Much joy - I'm feeling . . . Bountiful friends around me
now
Empty dreams abounding . . . Black pits pin me down . . .
The menace of hard years . . . No cheerful countenance can
be found

September 11- Sharing the Experience

Glued to the TV Like a forceful magnet . . . People from all
walks of life . . . Eyes filled with awe . . . Eyes filled with tears
Hearts beating fast . . . Creases of agony deep on each face
as we tried to understand what we heard . . . . And what we
saw on . . . September 11
Words would not come . . . Mindset - one of fear . . . Eyes with
disbelief as flames and smoke evolved . . . Buildings
collapsed . . .
Bodies dropping from the buildings and buried under tons of
metal and debris on . . . September 11
People running, people fainting, people sobbing
A melting pot we truly were as people carried people . . .
People helped people
White collared, blue collared, no collared, republicans,
democrats, males, females, gays, lesbians, catholics,
baptists, methodists, blacks, whites, hispanics,
asians, africans, young and old, rich and poor
Sharing the experience . . . Sharing the experience
on
September 11

She Is Who She Is

With me . . . She eats collard greens, cornbread, chitlins, chicken feet, fish heads, jelly cake and rice pudding galore.
Drank Kool-Aid by the gallons
Swept the dirt ground and watched the moon and stars through cracks in the roof. Emptied the slop jar at night and slept with four sisters and brothers. Her wardrobe was from the 5 and 10-cent store, Goodwill and neighbors.

With you . . . She drinks Alize, Hennessey, and café latte
Leg of lamb and T-bone steak. Dines with the town's elite . . .
Mansion at the top of the hill adorned with bling, bling and more bling . . . Smooth words flow from her lips . . . Grammar to perfection as she frequents Marshall Fields and Macy's
With me- With you, With me - With you, the same . . . yet different. Who can say?
For, she is who she is

Sitting On Your Throne

You sit like a King or Queen on your throne as if you had that place for years and more years and then . . . some more years.

You show no empathy as I waste time in the unemployment line, want my welfare check to be on time, want my home free of bugs and mice Sitting on your throne . . . . Sitting on your throne.

Your judgmental attitude shines brightly as you try to show me where I went wrong through theories I never knew. You explain my children as being the result of Freud's sexual energy . Not finishing high school on Piaget's cognitive development. My lack of drive as refuting Roger's self-actualization -through theories I never knew— through theories I never knew. Sitting on your throne . . . Sitting on your throne .

Unconditional positive regard to me—you never had. Absent from class when the professor said . . . unconditional positive regard—you must have. Unconditional positive regard—you never had. Approval of me you never had. Caring for me—you couldn't do. Sitting on your throne . . . Sitting on your throne.

Choices . . . I never had. Decisions . . . you say I can't make. Decisions about me . . . only you can make. Sitting on your throne . . . Sitting on your throne . . . .

Eye contact . . . you never make. Phone calls you never return. A few minutes you give to me to tell me of my bumps, mountains and barbed wire fences of life. Sitting on your throne . . .Sitting on your throne

68

Sizzling Love

Sizzling love is like no other.
It heals the sick
Comforts the weary
Encourages the hopeless
Calm the angry
Humbles the arrogant
Gives inner peace
Gives strength to the weak
Bring smiles to the sad and dejected
Uplifts the spirit
Makes the impatient patient
Is survival and hope during struggles
Softens the storms of life.
Sizzling love is phenomenal, beautiful and encouraging
Sizzling love is real.
Sizzling love is strength.

Skeletons

Skeletons in my closet won't go away
Returning at unexpected times,
trapped in a web.
The lies
The fornication
The crimes
The drugs
The gambling
The lust
The corruption
The jealousy
The backbiting
Like shadows following closely, darting in
and out
These skeletons just won't go away.

Splitting-up

Splitting up is lonely
Splitting up is sad
Splitting up is anger
Splitting up is silent
Splitting up is rejection
Splitting up is tearful
Splitting up is painful
Splitting up is frightening
Splitting up is devastating
Splitting up is expensive
Splitting up is final
Splitting up is hard to do when in love

Stand Still

Stand still . . .
While the birds sing
The crickets jump
The flowers bloom
Stand still . . .
As the thunder rolls
As the lightning flashes
And the wind howls
Stand still
While the clouds form
The rain falls
The sun shines
The seasons change
Stand still . . .
While tempers flare
Eyes roll
And tongues wag
Stand still . . .
In times of joy,
turmoil and grief
Stand still . . .
When relationships begin, end
and during sickness and health
Stand still . . .
When life begins
And life ends
Stand still . . . Stand still
Stand very still

Cause there's nothing you can do about it

Storms of Life

The storms of life are forever . . .

They make me . . .
stronger in faith to face the next storm
humble in knowing that I can't face the storms alone
compassionate for others during their storms.
patient during the duration of each storm
diligent in praying for strength during each storm.
insightful about God's work in sending storms
humane to others when they ask for help during storms

Storms of life are forever and forever

Strangers

Laughing, giggling, staring . . . a thing of the
past
Touching, feeling, caring . . . a thing of the
past
Cuddling, dancing, longing . . . a thing of the
past
Trusting, confiding, venting . . . a thing of the
past
'Cause we are strangers during the day
And strangers during the night

Stripped and Discarded

I was on top of the world . . . for a time that
seemed like eons.
Friends all around me, supporting me, loving me.
Kind words, accolades, kudos, gentle
strokes . . . . you name it.
My name and reputation—synonymous with high
regard and integrity.
Common in circles of the accomplished.
On cloud nine . . . I floated
with my head toward the sky .
Until I . . . Until I . . .
lost my touch due to mounted problems
that prevented me from thinking, doing, and becoming.

Once kind words . . . Now words of condemnation,
scorn, and ridicule.
King . . .Now a peon
My name now associated with deviance.
Now cold days, sleepless nights, and loneliness
as I realize how it feels to be stripped and discarded.

Teaching and Learning

Teaching and learning is . . .

Chaotic
Shouting
Chair banging
Energetic
Interactive
Unpredictable
Arrogance
Personable
Immaturity
Inspirational
And
Unique

A Woman . . . A Veteran

I left . . .
My husband and kids
My mom, dad, aunts, uncles and cousins
A familiar bed, kitchen and bathroom
A church family with praying warriors
Grocery stores and shopping centers
Pretty dresses and high heel shoes
I went . . .
To wearing uniforms and black boots
Cleaning barracks and cooking meals
decisions and assignments made for me
dirt roads and land mines
Flying planes and jumping from planes
Sailing ships
Shooting big guns
Carrying and fixing heavy equipment
Dragging the wounded to safety
Bandaging bloody wounds
Leading platoons and
to fight for my country
Who am I?
I'm a woman
and
I'm a veteran

The Color White

White is a color I use to love
until
I saw the horses with riders hiding their faces
beneath those beautiful white sheets
Until
I saw them directing the dogs to bite, and pointing the
powerful, stinging hose pipes that knocked us off our
feet
Until
I watched them hang people from trees like dark- fruit
and burning homes like trash . . . All in the name of
white supremacy

White is a color I use to love
use to love . . . but love no more

The Affair

She came into my husband's life
when days and nights could not be separated.
Hopelessness saturated his thoughts.
To her, he turned.
Completely hers . . . he became.
All for Love's Sake

Our Children . . . he dismissed.
Family and Friends . . . he ignored.
Church was a distant memory.
Body & Soul . . . he neglected.
All for Love's Sake

She was like a breath of fresh air for him
as he gave his time and treasures to her.
Made him laugh and laugh and laugh . . .
Then, sad and sad and sad . . .
Made his eyes glossy and piercing
Made him downright aggressive and bold.
All for Love's Sake

She wrapped him around her finger.
Controlled his mind and soul.
Who is she?
Crack-Cocaine

The Demented

Because I have . . .
Behavioral problems
Depression
Delirium
Anxiety
Sleeplessness
Hallucinations
And Delusions

Because I . . .
Wander away and get lost
Resist others
Wet my pants
Lose weight quickly and
Decline cognitively . . .
I am known as the demented.
    The demented

Life's Journey

As I close my eyes to the blackness of the night, I
see a multitude of stars thrown randomly in the
sky.
They remind me of my journey filled with sharp
nails and poisonous, deadly, keen edges

Yet coming at different times to allow me to
breathe, to breathe, to breathe and find
new energy for new jagged stones

Coping: A Daily Challenge

Intimate and intertwined few and far between
Almost hit by a car while distracted about issues
Jobless and hungry
Listening to backbiting, smiling people
Smiling when hurting inside
Feeling like 1 on a scale of 10
Throbbing pain in my body
Reflecting on the secret lives of my kids
Friendless
Lonely due to empty love
Headaches from thoughts of family secrets
Disorganized and out of control
A "to do" list that's never done
Problems that are never resolved
Unresolved grief that lingers

All of these and more seem to break me physically
and emotionally where I run the risk of internal
and external sores
And emotionally where peace of mind can only be
achieved by kissing the deep dark sea.

The Inmate

Anger . . .
Confusion . . .
Routine . . .
Financial burdens . . .
Shame . . .
Relationship problems . . .
Demoralized . . .
Low self-esteem . . .
Child-like state . . .
No brain needed . . .
Loneliness . . .
No contact . . . No love . . . Depression . . . Sleepless nights
  . . . All in the daily life of the inmate

The Involuntary Trip

No air could we feel
across our skin
No light could we see
No birds could we hear
No crickets jumping in
frivolous play
As we crossed that big ole dark sea
As we crossed that big ole dark sea

Only moans and groans in rhythm
Sighs of defeat, a constant pattern
Stares of desperation . . . a lasting memory
Movement prohibited by iron chains
Meshed together like canned sardines
As we crossed that big ole dark sea
As we crossed that big ole dark sea

Our bodies used to feed the fish
Bold night rodents roamed without fear
Kissing, chewing, sucking, dropping
Mutilating our bodies at will
As we crossed that big ole dark sea
As we crossed that big ole dark sea
As we crossed that big ole dark sea

Privileged

What if I am privileged? Don't be jealous . . .
Because I can get a loan when I have bad credit or
no credit
Buy a house without a bank account or get a pro-
motion without even applying

So, what if I am privileged?
Is it wrong that I don't have to work and I can afford to
have my nails, toes and hair fixed just
right and my children in dance, music and travel
abroad
What if I am privileged? Don't be mad
Because I don't have to go through mounds of
paperwork and interviews for admission to
the Ivy league schools
Because I can walk into a store, fill my purse with
merchandise with
out being suspected
Because I can buy a dress today, wear it tonight and
take it back the next day for a refund.
Yes, yes, yes . . . I am privileged
My name is privilege. That's just the way the world is
At least . . . My world

Trying Times

No more peace within the walls of our home.
Parents fighting each other and children fighting
Parents.
Incest and rape of family by family
cause we have become strangers and enemies.

Crack and meth is available like candy . . .
cooked in homes like meals where the aroma is
inhaled by both people and pets.

Gangs increasing their families
Tornadoes touched our house, your house, and other
houses leaving us stripped, empty and impoverished.

Hurricanes soaked our belongings, leaving
mold and mildew and keepsakes only in the mind.

The sun's heat made the ground hard as clay
where the veggies refused to come out.

Soldiers killed and wounded daily as a
testimony of greed and hate.

Terrorists willing to die in order to kill the enemy.
These are trying times

The Long Dark Night

I cry because of the long dark night
when all evils evade my territory.
Creeping in . . . Creeping out
Creeping in and out . . . whispering and touching
tipping and crawling in like the night rodents,
wrapping around me like a slippery snake.
The smell of old, the smell of old, clings heavily on
my nostrils
hard as a rock, hard as a rock
ready to invade, ready to invade my tiny hole
prodding, poking, prodding, poking until
the hole that never healed is raw,
loose and dangling
My silent screams exploded like rockets within me
Screams never heard by others—Screams never heard
by others,
Morning light, where are you?
Morning light seems no where in sight.
I cry because of the long dark night—the long long
dark night
Morning light, where are you?
Where are you?

The Missing Face

Quietly and loving he sat
No verbal expression needed
Communicating with eyes and movements
Patience far removed . . .
Trying to remember a face

Anger coming and going
Sadness like a shadow
Passion well hidden . . .
Trying to remember a face

Pain disguised by truancy,
Aggressiveness, drug and alcohol use
Concentration far removed
Hostility—a close friend
Probation officer—a close pal
Trying to remember a face

Thoughts of deception
Mountains of insecurity
Demoralized by society
Trying to remember a face
Trying to remember a face . . .
Of long ago

The Woes of Wars

Memories . . . never to be forgotten of the faces of
loved ones here today and gone forever.
Minds once calm, now replaying the pictures of explosive
bombs and flying body parts.

Eyes that saw the wonders of the world with hope-
ful anticipation, now flicker in darkness and pain.

Arms and legs replaced with steel as they learn to
walk again.

Memories . . . memories never to be forgotten
of families in tact now scattered like seeds.

Dreams of sugar plums, now dreams of bullets,
suicide bombs and disfigured bodies.

Memories . . . memories never to be forgotten
of sacrifices of faithful angels protecting our
country.
of cold nights and rodent infected tents,
of children begging for food and money,
with innocent eyes, but hiding bombs, and
of available women who shared their bodies.

Wars begin, end and start again
These memories are never to be forgotten.

Lust

My daddy yearned to see his lady on the other side of town
His face was twisted with anxiety as he paced the wooden
floors.
His eyes seem far away and filled with longing and
anticipation.
Sweat dripping like big tears on the floor.

When he could not take it any longer, he yelled
loudly at mama for darkening the toast and the
meat being too brown.

His rage was fierce, his eyes said hate and his
body jerked in quick motions as he knocked
mama to the floor when fleeing out the door.

All of this to quiet the yearning and lust of his body for his
lady on the other side of town.

The Power of Social Work

Feel the power of social work
Just feel the power of social work as we . . .
Recognize uniqueness in all God's children
Speak out against sexual and racial oppression
Fight for social justice
Respond to community needs

Just feel the power of social work
I feel the power of social work as we . . .
Individually and collectively strengthen individuals and
families
Use a code of ethics to guide us
Contribute to practice interventions
Develop theories and policies and
Use different helping approaches and techniques to
invite positive change

Just feel the power of social work
Feel the power of social work as we . . .
Spend hours helping one person
Travel from cities to rural Appalachia to help children,
women, the elderly, the poor, the uneducated,
and the disenfranchised

Feel the power of social work
Just feel the power of social work

The Reunion

They come from all corners of the earth
Gathering together, but misleading, superficially,
falsely.
They are friends and foes alike . . .
Pretend to be full of love and concern . . .
Crawling and darting from one to another . . .
Seeking fellowship but ending in alienation . . .
Determined to discover what life has dealt . . .
Filling their tubs with grease and more grease . . .
Consuming liquids that bring out their boldness
while stumbling about the floor and
revealing their very core.
Some show the enormity of guilt.
Some reveal incomprehensible hidden bitterness.
Some saw love they could never have.
Others had scars dealt by sin.

The Big Decision

To be or not to be
To be or not to be is the question
As the clock ticks and the days pass, I grow bigger
and bigger in the soft and warm safety of my
mother's womb. To be or not to be

To be or not to be is the question and the big decision.
The big decision of whether I am to be or not to be
born in this beautiful world.

Yesterday

Yesterday
I had a face tight and smooth,
Skin smooth as silk,
A flawless neckline,
Thick, coarse and healthy hair,
A strong heart,
A clear voice,
Clean fingers and toe nails,
Good health and few worries.

Today
I am wrinkled as a withered rose,
Hands that tremble continuously,
Feet that slide slowly,
Hoarse and cracked voice,
Lots of problems, bruises, and illnesses.

Today
All I have are memories of yesterday . . .
Of a good life.

The Tenant

Tenant . . . Tenant . . .
Where's the rent?
Come today . . .
Come tomorrow . . .
Come next week . . .

Tenant . . . Tenant . . .
Where's the rent?
Baby's sick . . . Broke my leg
Support didn't come

Tenant . . . Tenant . . .
Where's the rent?
Lost my job . . .
Been in jail . . .
This place is a dump
You shouldn't want any rent.

The Will

Siblings sit in quiet anticipation
to determine what place they hold
in the heart of the deceased.
Cliques form, chatter begins.
Anticipation of what's to come

Shush! Shush! The will is about to be read
The words in the will were like a knife in some ears
and love in others
as one was given more than others.
That can't be right . . . That can't be right
echoed from their mouths in disbelief . . .

Now . . .
Fingers point,
Silence is the mode,
Quiet politeness,
The closeness of childhood gone away.
No talk of love and unity . . .
but rudeness and accusations.
Seasons of history renewed . . . the good, the bad, the ugly
All because the will has been read.

Storms of Life

The storms of life are forever . . . .
They make us . . .
stronger in faith to face the next storm
humble in knowing that we can't face the storms alone
compassionate for others during their storms
patient during the duration of each storm
diligent in praying for strength during each storm
knowledgeable about miracles
insightful about God's work in sending storms
humane to others when they ask for help during storms.

    Storms of life are forever and forever

Time to Eat

It's time to eat but we don't have much.
Four, six, eight, ten little heads standing around,
wide eyed and hungry.
Five of these belong to me and the others to folks
down the road.
Time to go . . . time to go but they don't move cause
they're hungry and can smell the cornbread,
greens and fried chicken backs.
It's time to eat . . . but they won't leave.

Four,six, eight, ten little heads,
hunger showing in their eyes,
begging not to be sent away.
I felt a nudge at my heart and opened my door as
ten little heads jumped with joy as we shared the
cornbread, greens, juice from the greens and fried chicken
backs.
It suddenly didn't matter that five little heads belonged
to me and the others to folks down the
road . . . It didn't matter cause all the little heads
were hungry.

Trapped

I'm aching
for two arms, two hands, two legs
for ten fingers, ten toes,
two eyes, two ears
a brain, fortitude, wisdom and skill
I'm aching
to feel the wind on my cheeks
to taste the depths of delicious dishes
to feel the warmth of the human touch
to accept the love that may be offered
I'm aching
to be brave and smart
to make my own decisions
to triumph with skill
to have knowledge overflowing
to have the will to win
I'm aching
to know myself
to be armed for whatever challenges I face
to be great and bestow abounding deeds
to say what I want to say
to go where I want to go
to do what I want to do
. . . . . . .to do, to do, to do
I'm aching
. . . .to do.

Trauma Baby

My experiences leave me with no sense of self
Unavailable, inconsistent, undependable angel
Bruised, wounded, and abused
Explosive, toxic and poisonous
Lack of beauty and vitality
Fear, doubt and no trust
Bitterness and rejection
Sleepless nights
Suffering inflicted by my loved ones
Helplessness and hopelessness
Sadness, little enthusiasm
Anger, withdrawn, depressed,
Fear and uncertainty

No sensitive protective arms directing, guiding, teaching me
Hands that cripple and stifle me . . .
Keeping me from growing and developing into the greatness
I could be

Doctors, lawyers, nurses, policemen, judges, social workers
-
Stop being my silent partners . . . be my voice
For I am a trauma baby

I Fall Short

I'm afraid to challenge social injustice
I'm even afraid of the vulnerable and oppressed
I'm clueless about poverty, unemployment, and discrimination.
I'm out in left field when it comes to sexual harassment, sex- ism, racism and ageism that plague you daily.
I fall short
I do not respect your cultural and ethnic differences for . . .
I am the helper and you need my help.
You lack the ability to make your own decisions and determine your life's direction.
Your problems are many because you sit by idly and I refuse to enhance your capacity to address your needs.
I fall short
You are not my partner in any sense of the word.
You have no strengths that I can see that will help to restore and maintain your functional status or empower you.
I listen with one ear open while my mind is preoccupied since my loyalty is not to you.
My primary interest is me and mine.
I fall short
I'm educated and licensed to be the boss.
I've already spent too many hours in the classroom
No more study . . . No more training for me.
The techniques I know are used for all of you regardless of your problems.
I fall short
Don't tell me anything that you don't want me to share. Secrets of the heart will no longer be secrets of your heart.
I fall short, yes I fall short
Although I made a lot of promises as a social worker . . .
I fall short

Mixed Matched Shoes

Mixed matched shoes don't look or feel right

Won't let us dance through life together

Won't let us make our house a home

Won't let us laugh and love and play

Won't let us work together

Won't let us share our grief and pain

Because we are Mixed Matched shoes

We Are . . .

We are the young, the old, the sick, the needy

We are the brave, the resilient, the capable, the cream of
the crop

We are cooks, teachers, farmers, and factory workers,

shopkeepers, engineers, maids

beauty queens, movie stars, and more.

We are sisters, brothers, daughters, sons, aunts,

uncles, cousins, wives, husbands, mothers and fathers.

We are bitter sometimes due to life's blows.

We are happy sometimes because we feel blessed.

We are stared at—and stared at some more.

We are gentle, humble, and caring.

We are brave, conscientious, and proud.

We are . . . We are . . . We are . . .

THE PHYSICALLY AND MENTALLY CHALLENGED

Where Did My Love go?

I once loved to protect children

I once loved to protect the elderly

I once loved to advocate for the vulnerable

I once loved to advocate for the oppressed

I once loved to preserve families

I once loved to empower people

I once loved to develop relationships

What happened?

Where did my love go?

Like An Oak Tree

The mighty Oak Tree stands tall and firm
Never bending . . . Refusing to surrender to the storms of life
that beat and beat against it.
The root surely must be anchored deep and meshed like
welded steel.
It must be the powerful juices that run through its veins . . .
So potent to keep it strong, unshaken, and resilient.
Some people are like oak trees.

Stars

As I close my eyes to the blackness of night, I see stars thrown randomly in the sky. Some are close together in clusters while others are scattered all around in different places.

These stars remind me of my journey through life . . . a journey sometimes filled with calmness and joy and other times with sharp nails, stones and poisonous deadly edges coming at different times to allow me to breathe, to breathe and find new energy for new jagged stones.

You Forgot

You forgot to let your eyes see my blank stares and spacey look.

You forgot to let your ears hear my cries of hopelessness and despair.

You forgot to let your heart feel the deep pain of the demon that left me powerless.

You forgot to let your arms reach out to me when I felt weak and helpless.

You forgot to let your feet follow my whimpering sounds when my

body and soul were being violated.

You forgot that I was soul of your soul,

Bone of your bone,

Flesh of your flesh,

Blood of your blood,

Breath of your breath,

Protected by your skin and organs for 9 wonderful months

I hate you, hate you, hate you, hate you . . . because . . .

You forgot to be my mother

Issues

Issues in life are like trees with hundreds of
branches with different sizes, dimensions and weight
Branches swaying back and forth like feathers made of steel
. . . flaunting, teasing, and displaying their strength and
resilience by bending and bouncing back and refusing to
break despite life's storms and bruises.

Others so fragile they snap and break with the slightest
impact . . . void of inner strength. and support to hold on.

Their trunks, once beautiful with vibrant life are covered with
dark dripping mold and resin flowing from years of tears that
never seem to stop. All because of a life of stressful issues,
issues, issues.

Toxic and Untouchable

I was reminded to keep my distance, to respect
boundaries as I witnessed a plethora of human suffering
and tragedies.
My innate compassion, empathy, and desire tugged at my
inner soul and pulled on the strings of my heart like a violin
as I watched the scaley skin laced with sores and pus.
Dead skin had fallen over his coat like snow.

The disempowerment of my client was over-whelming as a
weak hand reached out for a human touch and not
the touch of cold thick latex.
My immediate instinct was to freeze in my steps
and to withdraw, but I was humbled and decided
to not ignore the limp hand.
I reached out and touched that frail hand that belonged to a
scared, angry and obviously decaying person.
I touched the untouchable . . . the demented . . . the toxic.
I'm glad I did because in doing so, I accompanied
a human being, a person, a breathing soul
through dark chaos and a painful existence.
I reached out and touched the toxic and untouchable.